The World of
HOUSE
PLANTS

The World of
HOUSE
PLANTS

Patrick A. Johns

NEW YORK

Photographic acknowledgments
Hamlyn Group Picture Library: endpapers, 2, 14, 33 top, 41 top, 41 bottom, 43 top, 45, 50 top, 51, 53 bottom, 54 left, 54 right, 59 bottom, 63 bottom, 64 top. Patrick Johns, Grayshott: 6, 7, 8 top, 8 bottom, 9, 10 top, 10 bottom, 11, 12, 13 top left, 13 top right, 13 bottom, 15, 16 top, 16 bottom, 17 top, 17 bottom, 18, 19 top, 19 bottom, 20, 21 top, 21 bottom, 22, 23 top, 23 bottom, 24, 25, 27, 28, 29, 30, 33 bottom, 34, 37 top, 37 bottom, 40, 43 bottom, 47, 49, 50 bottom, 52, 53 top, 55, 59 top, 62, 64 bottom. Harry Smith Horticultural Photographic Collection, Rettendon: 32, 39, 46, 56, 58, 60, 61. Michael Warren, Ipswich: 31, 35, 36, 38, 44, 48, 57, 63 top.

Copyright © 1982 The Hamlyn Publishing Group Limited
Reprinted 1983

First published in the USA in 1982
by Exeter Books
Exeter is a trademark of Simon & Schuster
Distributed by Bookthrift
Bookthrift is a registered trademark of Simon & Schuster
New York, New York

ISBN 0-671-05587-9

Printed in Italy

Contents

Happy Surroundings

Choosing the Plant: Points to Watch

Like most things in life, a cheap plant is not always a bargain. And yet an expensive one is no guarantee that your new plant will give the pleasure and joy expected. Having said that, there is no reason at all why the plant should not give satisfaction provided you bear in mind a few simple tips.

Leaves with brown spots and scorched edges are a sure sign that something is amiss.

A good healthy specimen will stand a far better chance than an ailing one. It usually pays to go to a retailer experienced in caring for house plants. He will know that most of them do not like spending their day outside, however pleasant the weather, in mid-winter. Nor do they like being wrapped in a paper sleeve for any length of time: the leaves like to see daylight, and let us face it, we like to see what we are buying.

Look for a plant free from pests like greenfly which cluster in groups or the mealy bug with its white waxy covering and brown scale insects resembling miniature tortoises. They all suck sap from the plant and will soon make it sickly. Some leaves are yellow by nature, but when they should be green, something is amiss and the plant is better avoided. Brown spots and scorched edges are warning signs too. Broken stems and leaves, withered flowers and dirty pots are all an indication of careless culture.

Turn the pot upside down to see if the roots are growing through the drainage holes, a sure signal that the plant needs potting on to a larger size container and may already be starving. Finally, ask the sales assistant for a pot plant sleeve to help protect your purchase on the journey home.

Choosing the Right Spot

Most of the plants which decorate our homes started off in very different surroundings: no doubt the nurseryman provided them with an atmosphere where temperature, light and humidity was controlled within fine limits. Before that, they were growing in congenial surroundings where nature intended them

to be. House plants do adapt themselves to a certain extent and it would be
a very unusual house that does not
provide suitable conditions somewhere.

Temperature
During their resting stage, plants usually
require a lower temperature; the same
can be said for the winter when growth
is not so active, and certainly most of
them prefer the daylight hours to be
warmer than the night. In winter they

may have no option, even when the room
is centrally heated during the day.

House plants will tolerate a con-
siderable variation but sudden fluc-
tuations should be avoided, otherwise
leaves will react by curling or by
developing spots and brown edges or by
dropping off altogether. Flower buds
often drop under these conditions too. It
is only fair to bring the plant inside the
room away from the window during cold
winter nights.

Healthy plants make a fine
display grouped together.

7

Most plants like a light position but take them away from the window when the nights are cold.

Few plants will put up with a draught, whether hot or cold. Obvious places are close to a doorway or an ill-fitting window frame, although it is surprising how draughty the stairs area can be on a cold night. On the other hand, very high temperature without correspondingly high humidity and good light intensity can be detrimental too.

Light

Light is essential for all house plants; the only difference is in the amount each sort prefers. Generally the darker leaved plants require less light, those with variegated leaves rather more and flowering subjects need a fairly high level but always shaded from strong sun.

In spite of the fact that some plants will tolerate low light levels, they all require sufficient for their needs to maintain healthy growth. Insufficient light results in weak, spindly growth drawn towards the source of light and pale, sickly leaves.

Natural light can often be supplemented by artificial light with the aid of fluorescent tubes, so that a very attractive feature can be made of perhaps an otherwise rather dull area. Some lights can get rather hot and damage the leaves; the same can be said for the plants stood too close to a window receiving full blast from the sun.

Humidity

Cactus plants have adapted themselves very well to arid conditions, as have others with tough leaves. The majority, however, prefer a certain amount of moisture in the air to prevent them from drying out and wilting. When that happens, the leaves are inclined to go brown around the edges.

Various methods can be adopted to provide humid atmosphere around the leaves: a daily syringe over with tepid water is ideal for some plants, except those with minute hairs growing from the surface. Alternatively the plant pot may be plunged in moist peat; for preference the less decomposed, light coloured peats are better because they are slightly more coarse and are less inclined to become waterlogged.

A container filled with pebbles kept moist with water filled to just below the surface is both functional and attractive. In all cases where a reservoir is used, do be sure that it is watertight and that the water level is below the surface to avoid uptake by the plant, unless that is intended of course.

Small stones scattered over the surface of the compost are attractive; they help to retain moisture too.

8

Tea Pots and Terrariums

There is no end to the number of different containers which may be used to enhance the beauty of your plant, and indeed the room too. A search through store cupboards will no doubt turn up interesting items, like old teapots and fish bowls. Equipment used in forgotten hobbies can be put to good use again : wine fermenting jars are ideal miniature greenhouses. Junk shops make good hunting grounds, where all sorts of interesting containers may be picked up for next to nothing.

Decorative containers and those with an unusual shape add interest when a plant has finished flowering. They may be arranged at different heights to provide a hanging garden effect, and enclosed containers such as bottles will reduce the watering required. Plants like to grow close to one another so it is a good idea to put several in the same vessel. Take care to select those plants needing the same conditions, otherwise they may be over or under watered.

Plants like to grow together. Choose the ones which require the same conditions and grow to different heights.

Above: Very large containers are best filled with loamy compost to support the plant over a number of years.

Right: Peat-based compost is ideal for small pots and bowls: it is clean and light to handle.

Pots and Bowls

The container may be filled with growing medium to support the plant, and in that case drainage material such as pebbles or baked clay granules are spread over the bottom to avoid waterlogging the plant when it is watered. The drainage aggregate should be at least 3 inches (7·5 cm) deep and it is a good idea to sprinkle charcoal over the surface to help keep everything sweet.

Large containers that are expected to grow the same plants on year after year, are filled with a loam-based compost (John Innes No. 2). Smaller containers which hold the plant for up to two years before moving them on, may be filled with a loamless compost based on peat. The difference here is that a loam-based compost will have in reserve certain plant foods such as boron and zinc; although a correctly made loamless medium has them to begin with, the plants may well have used them up by the end of two years. These trace element plant foods are not always easy to apply in the correct dose, and so for very long term use loam-based compost – but do ensure that it has been made up correctly using sterilized loam.

Large containers are better planted up in their permanent position because it is surprising how heavy they can be when they are filled with compost, especially one with soil included. It is more comfortable to plant up small bowls on the draining board or table. The plants to be moved on should be given a good drink while they are still in the original container, otherwise the rootball will not take up moisture from the new compost quickly enough. Lay a piece of old blanket or similar material over the drainage material in the bottom of the container. This will prevent the compost from washing down through. Now begin to fill up with the compost and place the plants as work proceeds. Carefully knock the plants from their existing containers and plant them so that they are at the same height as they were in the original pot, or just slightly below.

Remember to leave a space at the top of the container for watering. A certain amount of settlement will take place after the first watering, provided the compost has not been pressed down too firmly. A 2-inch (5-cm) space should be left for large containers. Moss-covered stone, or a piece of driftwood adds an artistic touch to the feature. Finally, the plants should be given a watering to settle them in their new quarters.

A wide range of plants is suitable for pots and bowls and contrasting plants make an interesting piece, for example *Sanservieria* with *Ficus radicans*, or *Dracaena* with *Scindapsus*. For the larger container, the Fiddle leaved fig, Kentia palm, Rubber plant, Swiss cheese plant and *Schefflera* do well.

Instead of planting directly into the container, another use is as an outer for the plant pot itself; the house plants can thus be rearranged from time to time.

Contrasting shapes and colours make an interesting feature.

Troughs

Waterproof troughs may be planted in the same way as pots and bowls and used, for example, as room dividers. Tall plants or climbers like *Hedera* are ideal; also the Kangaroo vine, *Philodendron* and *Scindapsus*. Try to include a wide range of different leaf shapes and colours.

Troughs can be used to accommodate plants in their own pots and this is a very good idea when individual plants are relatively short-lived: they can be removed from the collection without disturbing the others. Stand the pots on pebbles to avoid waterlogging: they may be packed around with moist peat to help raise humidity amongst the plants.

Bottle Gardens and Terrariums

All manner of containers may be brought into use here provided they will transmit sufficient light – and that rules out dark glass bottles. Acid carboys are ideal but take care to wash them out several times with detergent and tepid (not hot) water. Fermenting jars, brandy snifters or an aquarium all make suitable vessels for a mini landscape.

Bottles with a small opening at the top are not difficult to manage, aided by a few simple tools. A small spoon tied to a long stick is ideal for making planting holes, an old fork for raking the surface of the compost, and a cork pushed on the end of a stick for tamping and firming

Relatively short-lived plants can be plunged complete with their own pot into a larger container.

roots will be needed. Finally, two short lengths of soft wire tied to the end of a stick makes an ideal grip for lowering plants into position.

First place a layer of clean pebbles or burnt clay granules – they can be purchased from garden centres – over the base. Then sprinkle charcoal over the pebbles. A piece of blanket cut to size will keep the compost from fouling the drainage material below. Next carefully trickle in the compost which will run easier if it is a little on the dry side. Use a piece of stiff paper or kitchen foil to make a funnel so that the compost will go through the neck of the bottle without making the sides dirty. Aim to fill approximately one third of the container with compost so that there will be sufficient for the plants.

Take the plants from their container and gently roll them on a flat surface, or squeeze in the palm of the hand so that the roots form a cylinder which can be gripped by the soft wire tool and lowered into the hole made by your spoon. Then tamp the compost around the root with the cork.

Choose slow growing plants, and so far as bottle gardens are concerned it is better to avoid flowering plants because their fallen petals are sometimes difficult to remove. Suitable plants include *Adiantum*, *Begonia rex*, Bromeliads, *Chamaedorea*, *Ficus radicans*, *Hedera*, *Maranta*, *Peperomia* and *Pilea*. And for terrariums *Anthurium scherzerianum*, *Aphelandra*, *Codiaeum*, *Coleus*, *Fittonia*, *Impatiens*, *Kalanchoe*, *Maranta*, *Pachysandra*, *Peperomia*, *Pilea*, *Saintpaulia* and *Streptocarpus*.

Water the plants and then leave the container for two or three weeks before covering over the top.

Above left: Fermenting jars make ideal terrariums.

Above: A piece of blanket or capillary matting will keep the compost from fouling the drainage material below.

Left: Gently squeeze the roots so that they fit through the small opening. Firm the compost with a cork fixed to the end of a stick. Slow-growing plants are the best ones for terrariums.

13

Trailing plants are ideal for
suspended containers.

Hanging Baskets

Trailing plants in particular look very attractive in suspended containers. Special pots with drip trays attached may be purchased to avoid water dropping on to objects below. Given the choice, peat-based compost is more suitable than loam because it is lighter. Even so, loamless compost can be heavy when wet and therefore the container should be suspended from an appropriate place.

The atmosphere around suspended plants tends to be drier, so they should be inspected more frequently and watered accordingly. Suitable plants for hanging baskets include Asparagus fern, *Chlorophytum*, *Hoya*, *Hedera*, *Philodendron*, *Saxifraga*, *Schlumbergera*, *Scindapsus* and *Tradescantia*.

Hydroculture

House plants may be purchased already potted in special containers filled with an inert material like baked clay granules. Special fertilizer is used so that the plants need feeding only every six months or so. The main advantage of the system is that the plants require much less attention than those potted in conventional compost.

Plants growing in ordinary compost may be converted to hydroculture with the aid of special kits purchased from garden centres. These kits contain a special pot with water seep holes, clay granules and fertilizer, and a float cylinder is often included to see when watering is necessary.

It is most important that every scrap of existing compost is carefully washed from the roots, otherwise the roots will rot away. The plant should then be suspended in the container with the baked clay granules allowed to trickle in around the roots. Fill the pot with granules and then sprinkle the recommended amount of special fertilizer over the surface. Then fill the container to within one third of the top with tepid water; it is most important to use mains tap water so that the proper chemical reaction takes place with the fertilizer.

The container should be allowed to go almost dry before more water is applied so that air will circulate around the root zone.

Special clay granules can be purchased for hydroculture.

Fun Plants for the Family

Above: The Venus fly trap feeds on small insects.

Right: Sow a packet of mixed seed for a fine collection of cacti and succulents.

All plants are fun to grow but some have that unique difference. Perhaps they eat insects, or suddenly fold their leaves to frighten pests away which would otherwise eat them. Some succulents are so well camouflaged that they look like stones. Imagine gathering your own peanuts or picking your own oranges to flavour a refreshing drink!

Most of these plants are easy to grow and a good number may be germinated in the airing cupboard, provided the pot is enclosed in a polythene bag to keep the compost moist.

Venus Fly Trap (Dionaea musipula) The insectivorous plant secretes sugary sap over the surface of its saucer-shaped trap. When insects land on the surface to feed, the trap suddenly closes to catch the insect which is then slowly dissolved.

Sow the seed on peaty compost but do not cover the seed with compost. Keep moist and at a temperature of between 70–80°F (20–25°C).

Sensitive Plant (Mimosa pudica) The leaves suddenly fold up when they are touched. Young plants are most sensitive so a pinch of seed should be sown every six months or so. Seed germinates faster when it is soaked in hot water for 15–20 minutes before sowing.

Sow the seed on the surface of the compost and germinate in a temperature of 70°F (20°C). Pot off singly when the plants reach the stage at which they are large enough to handle.

Peanut (Arachis hypogaea) These are nicely shaped plants with yellow pea like flowers. The flowers push under the compost to produce peanuts.

Take the nuts from their husky case and sow them in compost at 70°F (20°C). Roasted peanuts will not grow!

Cacti and Succulents, including Pebble Plants (Lithops) Sow a packet of mixed seed on the surface of sandy compost and watch the different sorts of plants grow.

Pebble plants are aptly named, because they do look just like stones. Sow the seed in a temperature of 70–80°F (20–25°C). When the plants are large enough, carefully transplant them into sandy compost and scatter small stones or pebbles amongst them.

Orange Orange pips sown in peaty compost and kept at 70°F (20°C) will soon germinate to grow into fine bushy plants. They do not mind being on the cool side during winter but really like a nice light position, shaded from strong summer sun.

The plants will eventually bloom and the sweetly scented flowers should be syringed over each day to help set the fruit.

Date Palm Put the date stones in a bag of moist peat in the airing cupboard. When the small white root emerges, carefully pot singly in compost. The Date palm makes an attractive plant with its ribbed leaves – but it is unlikely that you will gather fruit from a palm growing in the house!

Avocado Pear The large stone may be germinated in an egg cup or glass filled with water, or directly in compost in a flower pot. Either way, it is likely to take a long time unless a small piece of the tough skin is removed first.

It is a very handsome plant for the home.

Pineapple Cut off the tuft of leaves from the top of a ripe fruit, together with the woody portion of fruit just below. Place the cutting on moist sand in a dish. Provided the atmosphere is warm, roots will grow from the base.

Pot the plant into compost and keep at 60°F (15°C) or above. Temperatures around 90°F (33°C) are required for the plant to produce ripe fruit.

The date palm makes an attractive plant for the home.

New plants can be grown from the top of a pineapple fruit.

New Plants from Old

Plant propagation is a fascinating subject and there is a great sense of satisfaction in raising new plants – whether to replace old ones, add to the collection, or to give away as presents.

The recommended method for each particular plant is given in the A-Z of Popular Flowering and Foliage House Plants and the degree of success depends on how the material is prepared. All plants used for propagation should be healthy.

Cuttings

A cutting is any part of the plant taken from the parent and encouraged to grow its own roots. The Busy Lizzie, for example, will grow roots from the base of a shoot tip snapped from the end of the parent stem. The cutting should remain turgid and the best way to ensure that it does is to insert the stem in moist peaty compost, or a glass of water.

Tip cuttings are approximately 2–3 inches (5–7·5 cm) long and cut below a leaf joint. The lower leaves are removed so that only clean stem is inserted in the compost. Rooting is aided by dipping the base into rooting hormone powder, available from garden centres and stores. The type of compost is important: it should be free draining and free from pests and diseases. John Innes seed compost or a proprietory loamless compost is ideal.

Plants like the ivy produce stems which may be cut up between the leaf joints. Each cutting will have a leaf and bud, plus the portion of stem. The end of the stem may be inserted in compost or placed on top, pegged down with a short loop of thin wire.

Leaf stalk cuttings from plants like the

Soft shoots taken from a plant will root. Large floppy leaves may be reduced.

Left: Plants like *Streptocarpus* and *Begonia* will grow new plants from their fleshy leaves.

Saintpaulia and *Peperomia* produce roots and small plants from the base of the stalk. These cuttings are made by removing a leaf complete with stalk from the parent; the stalk is then reduced to $\frac{1}{2}$ inch (12 mm) long and put in compost up the base of the leaf blade.

Parts of leaves can be made into cuttings. The leaf is removed from the parent and placed on a clean surface. Take a sharp knife and cut the leaf across into strips each approximately 2 inches (5 cm) wide. Plants like the *Gloxinia* and *Streptocarpus* are good examples: they have fleshy leaves with a strong main vein. *Begonia rex* is yet another example, and with this plant the leaves may be cut up into the size of postage stamp squares. In each case, the leaf section is best inserted edge on in the compost to avoid drying out.

Always keep the compost moist without being too wet; a polythene bag enclosing the container and cuttings is useful, provided it is supported with a stick to prevent the sides and top from touching the cuttings.

Division

Plants like *Sansevieria* grow suckers, or toes from the root zone. These are easily divided from the parent by carefully knocking the rootball from the pot. The sucker, complete with its own root system, is then potted up singly.

The new plant should be kept well shaded for a few days: light misting over with clear water helps establishment too.

Above: Daughter plants are sometimes produced by suckers growing from the root zone. Pot them off singly to make a new plant.

19

Folded paper is a convenient aid for sowing small seed.

Seed

Many house plants can be raised from seed. It is a comparatively inexpensive way to build up a collection, although it does take rather longer; flowering plants take longer to reach maturity.

Fill the container with seed sowing compost, either John Innes or a peat-based medium will do. Give the container one or two sharp taps on a solid surface, strike off the top with a straight edge and then lightly firm. The surface of the compost should be level without pits, otherwise some of the seeds may be too deep and will not germinate.

Lightly scatter the seeds so that they fall evenly and are well spaced out: very small seeds like *Begonia* may be mixed with clean, dry sand to help distribution. Not all seeds require covering and it is usually advisable to leave very small seeds bare on the surface. In the case of larger seeds, it is a good rule of thumb to cover them with compost to the depth of twice their diameter.

When moist compost is used, it may not be necessary to water the compost, provided it is covered with a sheet of glass or polythene until the seedlings are through. If watering is necessary, immerse the container to half its depth in a bowl of water rather than apply from the top, otherwise the seeds may be washed away.

When germination takes place, carefully transplant the seedlings before they get too large.

Doctor's Advice

House plants are sometimes subject to upsets just like any other member of the household. Give them the correct diet with a drink when they should have one, clean them if necessary and put them in a position where they are comfortable and they will present few problems.

Watering

It is true to say that a great many plants are killed by either too much or too little moisture. Look for your plant in the A-Z of Popular Flowering and Foliage House Plants to see its exact requirements; here it is sufficient to say that the majority of plants like to be kept moist without having their roots in a state of perpetual wetness.

Water from below whenever possible by standing the pot in water until the surface of the compost is moist. Deionized water from the pharmacy, or clean rain water, is satisfactory, but there is no reason why mains tap water should not be used for many.

Apply water when the compost feels dry to the touch; peat-based compost is much lighter to pick up when dry and it is often a lighter colour too.

Remember that plants should be given less water from October to March when growth is not so active.

Feeding

Little and often is the general rule when plants are in active growth, which usually means from April to September. Special house plant food may be purchased from garden centres and stores. It usually contains rather more nitrogen than other nutrients which is fine for foliage plants

Water from below, and when the surface of the compost is moist, the pot should be stood out to drain.

Use house plant food to keep the plant growing happily.

and flowering plants too. The flowering ones do, however, respond to a feed now and again with rather more potash: tomato fertilizer is ideal and it often contains magnesium to help keep the leaves healthy.

Avoid feeding a diseased plant; it will only make things worse. Newly potted plants seldom need feeding for the first few weeks after moving on and fertilizer, however dilute, should never come into contact with the leaves unless it has been made especially for the purpose.

Cleaning Leaves

Small pores in the leaves are used by the plant to take in and give off carbon dioxide and oxygen. When the pores are blocked, the plant is unable to function properly: not too much of a problem when the plant is growing out of doors, because the rain is able to wash them off. Indoors, however, it is different and the plant will appreciate cleaning. Tough shiny leaves may be wiped over with a damp cloth, or a leaf shine aerosol is a convenient way of making them look smart. Hairy leaves are better lightly brushed with a soft artist's brush.

Potting on

Sooner or later, the existing container will become full of roots. To prevent the pot becoming root bound, resulting in a starved, unhealthy plant, a larger container will be required. Signs that indicate potting on is needed are when roots grow out from the drainage holes and when the plant has an abnormal thirst for water. It is far better to repot before the symptoms appear, because by then the plant is already suffering.

Gently knock the plant from its container and inspect the root system. When you can see the roots beginning to turn on the outside of the ball, the time has come to move the plant on. Choose a container that is only slightly larger than the existing one. Make sure it is clean and dry, then place a small quantity of compost over the base of the pot: there should be no need for drainage material such as broken crocks or roughage with well made, modern composts.

Position the rootball in the middle of the pot without disturbing the roots, and then trickle the compost down the sides. Lightly press the compost down with the fingers from time to time and finish off by giving the base of the pot one or two sharp taps on a solid surface. A gap should be left at the top of the pot for watering. Finally, give the pot a thorough watering and provided the root was moist when removed from the previous pot, the moisture will penetrate the rootball without just draining down the sides.

Plants on Holiday

The chances are that our plants will look and feel as good as we do when we return from holiday, provided we have taken the right precautions before leaving.

A larger container will be needed when you see the roots.

22

Left: The use of a capillary wick enables the plant to water itself.

Check them all over for pests, diseases, damaged leaves and faded flowers. Give them a feed after making sure they are moist at the root. The lack of moisture is going to be the main problem during periods of absence. Fortunately, there are many ways to avoid the problem.

The easiest method for pots which can be moved is to insert a special capillary wick into the drainage hole. These sticks of compressed paper are purchased from garden centres and stores. The pots are then stood on bricks or upturned flower pots in the sink or bath. Provided the end of the wick is immersed in water, the plant will take up just the right amount to keep the compost moist.

Alternatively the plant pots can be given a good watering and then plunged in moist peat: as long as they are shaded from strong light and kept cool, no harm will come to them for a short while.

Holidays taken during November to March may present more of a problem, especially when the weather is very cold at home. There is always the chance of a sudden cold snap and it would be as well to make some provision for the plants.

Pests

Plant parasites can multiply at an alarming rate in the snug conditions of the house. Fortunately there are some very efficient insecticides we can use and they have been manufactured for use in the home. The most convenient are aerosols: only a very short burst is necessary, hardly enough to see and certainly not enough to wet the leaf.

Sucking pests like greenfly and white-fly puncture the skin and suck out the sap. This causes stunted and often puckered growth. Use 'Kerispray', Derris Liquid or Ortho Indoor Plant Insect Spray.

Above: Greenfly feeds on the sap of plants, often causing stunted growth. The pest should be sprayed with an insecticide.

23

Plant pests like mealy bugs suck sap and secrete 'honeydew' which attracts sooty mould. They should be controlled by using an insecticide made for home use.

Scale insects, like small brown tortoises and mealy bugs covered in their white wax, suck sap too; again 'Kerispray' can be used, or Malathion. Scale insects sometimes attach themselves to the main vein of the leaf when they can be removed with a fingernail.

The small Sciarid fly has become a real problem. It resembles a midge and hovers around the compost to find a home for its eggs. When they hatch, the maggots feed on the minute root hairs causing the plant to wilt. The maggots are killed by a root drench of spray strength 'Sybol 2', 'Lindex', Liquid Derris or Ortho Lindane.

Red spider mites, which are hardly visible with the naked eye, cause silver or yellow specks to appear on the leaf. In severe infestations, secreted webbing covers the leaves and shoots. Try to maintain a humid atmosphere and spray the plants with clear water each day. Liquid Derris, Ortho Rotenone Spray or 'Kerispray' may be used but some strains of the pest are very persistent.

Diseases and Disorders

These problems usually result because of poor cultural conditions. Starting with the root, it is no wonder that rot sets in if ordinary unsterilized garden soil is used; or too much fertilizer so that it scorches the roots. Water from an uncovered water butt is full of plant diseases.

Flower and leaf spotting is often caused by plant diseases that gain a foothold when the air is stagnant or too humid. Spots are just as likely to appear after water has been splashed about, particularly when the leaf is in full blast of the sun. The infected parts should be removed, otherwise fluffy grey mould will no doubt appear to infect other parts of the plant.

Mildews on the plant suggest that the roots have been allowed to dry out too much so that a check to growth has occurred. Dryness at the root also gives rise to brown spots and marked leaf edges, though this can be caused by the incorrect use of leaf shine and other aerosols as well.

The lack of feeding causes premature leaf fall after they have turned yellow, and a very dry atmosphere has the same result.

There is no reason why any of these things should happen with a little care and attention, although that may be easier said than done!

Brown or yellow spots on the leaves may be caused by dry compost around the roots, incorrect use of aerosol sprays or draught.

An A-Z of Popular Flowering and Foliage House Plants

Section 1: Flowering House Plants

Anthurium (Flamingo flower; Tail flower) An interesting plant, for its bright red flowers look almost unrealistic with their plastic-like spathe. *Anthurium andreanum* has large flowers which are often grown commercially for cutting; *A. sherzerianum* produces smaller flowers and is a smaller plant but easier to grow in the home.

Originating in tropical America, the plants prefer good light and shading from strong sun. Humidity is important so that the pot may be stood on a tray of moist pebbles and spraying the leaves with clear water from time to time is beneficial; in hard water areas however, deposits are sometimes left on the leaf which may be difficult to remove. These plants like to be watered freely from May to September, with the compost kept just moist from October to April. A minimum temperature of 55°F (13°C) is needed.

Seed germination is not always easy; it needs to be reasonably fresh and so it is usually more convenient to secure new plants by removing them from the parent. The young plants will have their own roots intact and are potted up into a peat-based compost right away.

Azalea (Indian azalea) Provided the natural light was good and there was room for just one house plant, the Indian azalea would be a good choice. The spectacular flowering extends over a long period through the darkest months. After flowering, the plant prefers the conditions out of doors until late August, making room inside for an alternative.

Azalea simsii (Rhododendron) will keep growing larger from year to year provided it is kept moist but not too wet and fed every other week. Overwatering and too much plant food will cause the leaves to drop. Acid conditions are required so

The Indian azalea is a very showy plant, flowering over a long period. Azaleas may be kept from year to year.

Keep Shrimp plants well watered during warm weather. A feed each week during the summer also keeps them healthy.

only boiled rain water or deionized water from the pharmacy should be used.

When the plant outgrows the container it is potted on into a slightly larger pot, using sphagnum peat. Feed with house plant food every ten days until the flower buds show colour.

Take the plant indoors during late August and syringe over with clear water each day for one month. Feeding should stop when the flower buds have developed.

Beleperone (Shrimp plant) Looking at the Shrimp plant when it is in flower it is easy to see how descriptive the common name is; especially the pink leafy bracts of *Beleperone guttata*. There is the yellow bract form too, favoured by flower arrangers. The true flowers are those white open-ended tubes growing between the bracts.

Despite the decorative value of the bracts, it really does pay to remove at least some of them as soon as the last true flower has withered. This will ensure further new growth to produce more flowers later on. Some of the shoots may be used for cuttings should additional plants be required.

Shrimp plants take up a lot of moisture during summer so the roots should be kept moist and a feed each week helps them along. Drier and somewhat cooler

conditions are required from October to March, although the temperature should not drop below 55°F (12°C). A feed once a month will be quite adequate during the dull months, because little if any growth will be made.

Emanating from Mexico, the plant enjoys a position in good light, especially so from October to March when the days are short and often dull.

Bougainvillea (Confetti flower) Given a minimum temperature of 45°F (7°C) and a sunny, draught-free position this climbing shrub from Brazil will produce more than enough flowering shoots. The real beauty is not in the actual flower which is rather insignificant, but the vivid bracts. They come in a wide range of colours with different varieties from deep purple, through mauve to red, orange and yellow.

Left to its own resources, the plant would soon create a mini jungle. February is a good time to take things in hand by cutting back the main stem by one third. Side shoots should be reduced to two leaf buds at the same time. The stems which grow from these buds may be trained around wire hoops pushed into the flower pot.

Feeding should commence after pruning in February: every other week will suffice until active growth commences, then increase to once per week during the following months to August. The compost needs to be uniformly moist until September, when less water is given so that the pot is on the dry side of moist for the rest period until the end of the following February.

Cuttings are not always easy to root; June is the best time of the year to take them, when the stem is not too soft. The shoots should be approximately $2\frac{3}{4}$ inches (7 cm) long and cut below the leaf joint. Dip the cut end into rooting hormone powder and then insert in a peat-based compost. The container and cuttings may then be put into a polythene bag to conserve moisture.

Browallia Here is a very pretty plant for the price of a packet of seeds. Bright blue flowers are produced over a long period some five or six months after sowing the seed. There is also a variety which produces white flowers.

The plants themselves will withstand temperatures down to 45°F (7°C) so they are ideal for growing through the cold, dark months, especially now that there is a variety 'Marine Bells' that will tolerate poor light. It has blue flowers and will grow to around 18 inches (45 cm) tall.

As the seed needs light to germinate properly it should be sown on the surface of a peaty compost without covering. A temperature of 60–65°F (16–18°C) is necessary and the seeds should germinate within three weeks. Seedlings are moved into flower pots when they are large enough to handle. Seed sown in March or April will produce plants to flower in September and seed sown in June or July provides February to April flowering plants.

When the plants are 3 inches (7·5 cm) tall, pinch out the tip of the shoot so that side branches will be encouraged to grow and produce more flowers. Generally,

Train the stems around wire hoops to keep *Bougainvillea* within bounds.

Colourful *Calceolarias* require cool conditions to extend the flowering period.

Opposite page: Remove faded flowers before they form seed pods and the Italian bell flower will produce many more flowers.

the plants grow better when they are given a position in good light.

Calceolaria (Slipper flower) This South American plant much prefers cool conditions and will not come amiss at 50°F (10°C): the flowers will last longer and the plant will be altogether more healthy than when conditions are too hot. Yellow leaves are a sure sign that too much water has been given and it would be as well to hold back so that the pot compost stays evenly moist without being too wet. The other point to bear in mind for sturdy, healthy foliage is to keep the plant in a light position.

The unusual puffy flowers of *Calceolaria herbeohybrida* come in a good range of different colours. Plants already in bloom can be purchased from garden centres or stores; alternatively seed may be sown in July or August to flower the following year. The seed is very small and care should be taken to sow thinly. Do not cover the seed with compost because light is required for germination. Moisture is needed too and the best way to moisten the compost without disturbing the seed is to stand the pot in a container of water until the surface is moist. A temperature of 61°F (16°C) is satisfactory for seed germination.

Campanula (Italian bell flower) The plant originally came from southern Europe, as the common name suggests. Good light and cool conditions are required for the best results; in fact provided the plant is not actually frozen stiff it will be quite happy.

Campanula isophylla is a trailing plant with bluebell-shaped flowers that seem to go on and on, provided the faded ones are removed before they develop into seed pods. There is also a white flowered kind known as 'Alba'.

A great deal of energy is used to produce lots of flowers, so as soon as buds show it pays to give house plant food each week and to ensure that the compost does not dry out. The plant can be saved after flowering by keeping the compost just moist, without being too wet.

Sow seed in March or April for new plants; alternatively cuttings can be taken from non-flowering shoots.

Cattleya The flowers are amongst some of the most alluring yet these are some of the easiest plants to grow. There are many orchids and a good number produce flowers which last for ages. This one was found in South America and named after the English botanist W. Cattley.

Many exotic orchids can be grown in the cool; their flowers last for weeks.

Opposite page, top: Keep the roots moist but avoid feeding once Pot chrysanthemums begin to flower.

Opposite page, bottom: Take care to water the Ash plant properly otherwise the leaves wilt when the roots are too wet.

Contrary to a wide held belief, high temperatures are not necessary and the plants are quite happy with 50°F (10°C) from October to February and 60°F (15°C) for the remainder of the year. It is most important to avoid overwatering at all times, otherwise too many leaves will grow at the expense of flowers. This is why orchids are often grown in hanging baskets and they look delightful when suspended by macramé. Excess water can then easily drain away, preferably into a receptacle below the basket. Special orchid compost with ingredients to promote good drainage can be purchased, or made up at home by mixing 2 parts osmunda fibre to 1 part sphagnum moss, by volume.

Although annual replanting is undesirable, there will come a time when a larger container becomes necessary. Those plants which flower during March and July should be replanted immedi-ately after flowering. Those flowering from August to February are replanted in March. When extra plants are required, roots may be divided up at planting time.

Place the plants in good light but shade from strong sun. A daily misting over from May to August is appreciated and watering is increased when the flower buds appear. The plant will look for a rest after flowering – reduce watering so that the compost is barely moist. Overhead spraying should cease altogether.

Chrysanthemum (Pot mum) Once traditionally grown as cut flowers for the end of the year and especially for Christmas, these plants are now adapted to grow all year round and as dwarf pot plants too. This is achieved by treating the young plants with growth regulating chemicals and by shortening the day-light hours artificially. The technique is not difficult although best left to the commercial grower with the necessary equipment who can produce the plant up to the stage when colour is showing in the bud.

The flowering period is extended considerably by maintaining a fairly low temperature and 50°F (10°C) is ideal. The compost in the pot should be kept moist without being too wet. It is not necessary to feed the plant once colour is showing in the flower bud.

Tempting though it may be to plant the contents of the pot in the garden after flowering, it is seldom worthwhile: the resulting plants often produce long spindly shoots without flowers, or if flowers do appear they will probably coincide with frosty weather.

Cineraria (Ash plant) The plant derived its name from the grey ash colour underneath the leaves and the fact that it originated in the volcanic Canary Islands.

It is prone to overwatering which causes the leaves to droop, and since wilting leaves usually indicate that a plant is dry at the root, there is a temptation to provide yet more water. Incorrect watering often gives rise to an attack of mildew which causes silvery marks on the leaves.

Seed is sown in peat-based or John Innes No. 1 loam compost, near 55°F (13°C). When the small seedlings are just large enough to handle, they are carefully moved singly one to each 3-inch (7·5-cm) flower pot. Clay pots are better than plastic because they are less likely to be overwatered: the clay evaporates a certain amount of moisture from the side of the pot and the pot may be tapped to see if the compost inside is dry, when it will ring; a dull thud means that the roots are still wet. Sufficient water should be given as required to moisten the compost all through to the bottom of the pot.

When the small pot is full of roots, the plant may be moved on to a 5-inch (12·5-cm) pot, using a peat-based compost again, or John Innes No. 2. The plants will be looking for extra nutriment after about four weeks from potting and house plant food is ideal. Feeding should cease when the flower buds begin to show colour.

Cinerarias are all the better for being cool and there is no reason why they should not be put outside for the warmer months. Provided the temperature is above 46°F (8°C) the plant will be happy. They like to be syringed over with clean water each day during hot weather.

Cigar plants like to be kept cool. They are easily raised from seed or by cuttings.

Opposite page: Grow the Poinsettia on for another year; short days will be necessary to encourage flowers again.

Sow seed in May for plants to flower the following Christmas, and early August for the following Easter.

Cuphea (Cigar plant) *Cuphea ignea* is a novel plant with its red tubular flowers which extend over a very long period from May to December.

The plant can withstand low temperature down to 45°F (7°C) without coming to any harm. Good light is required to avoid long straggly growth, although this Mexican does like to be shaded from strong sun.

New plants are raised easily from seed, or cuttings may be taken from non-flowering shoots in April and May.

Dipladenia The plant will grow to 15 ft (4·5 m) tall in its natural surroundings in Brazil. *Dipladenia splendens* with very attractive pink flowers can easily be kept within bounds as a house plant by training the stems on wire hoops pushed into the pot. These stems are cut back to three buds after flowering, or when a large plant is required, they may be cut back half way.

New plants are raised by taking stem cuttings in June, July or August and the plants are then grown on in a temperature of at least 55°F (13°C) for best results.

Euphorbia pulcherrima (Poinsettia) Many thousands of these Mexican plants are produced each year for the Christmas season. There is no reason why the plant should not give pleasure well into the new year provided it is kept snug and warm. Poinsettias are very prone to root rot and leaf fall when the temperature drops below 60°F (15°C). Overwatering will cause the same problems and the plant does like to be kept in a light place when flowering to avoid yellow leaves.

Those fresh green leaves and cheering red bracts stand a better chance when the plant is kept away from draughts, open fires and radiators. Very dry compost will cause leaf drop and when water is needed the chill should be taken off first.

The plant may be grown on in the second year, though unfortunately the bracts do not always colour up in time for Christmas unless the plant is given special treatment. This treatment starts when the plant has finished flowering by reducing watering; the stems are cut back to one third of their previous length. When side shoots appear start feeding the compost with house plant food and continue every other week from July to the end of September.

Long nights are needed for the leaf-like bracts to form and colour so that the plant must be kept in complete darkness for at least 13 hours in each 24. Provided a warm temperature at least 60°F (15°C) is maintained there is a fair chance that bracts will colour approximately 14 weeks after the long nights have started: mid September should be right for Christmas.

Fuchsias make attractive house plants and can be grown in pots or hanging containers. Cut the stems short each year to keep them tidy.

Exacum (Arabian violet; Persian violet) *E. affine* is an annual plant from Socotra Island off the east coast of Africa. It makes a very attractive house plant when grown from seed sown in August; smaller plants may be grown by sowing the seed in March. Either way, sweetly scented flowers are produced through June to September.

The pot compost should be kept moist and a feed each week is beneficial from May to September. A position in good light but shaded from strong sun is appreciated.

Fuchsia There is a trend towards the small flowered kinds and they make ideal house plants for a light window. Bushy growth is encouraged by pinching out the shoot tip from time to time. The shoot tips may be used to produce new plants.

The flowering period of these Central and South American plants extends from May to October. House plant food should be given each week during the growing season; a moist compost is needed otherwise flower buds will drop before they open. During November to

March the plant should rest by keeping the pot on the dry side in cool conditions.

Gloxinia *Sinningia speciosa* from Brazil is a very showy plant with no shortage of bright flowers of many shades in different varieties. Plenty of light – but shaded from strong sun – and moist compost with a feed each week from May onward will prolong flowering.

After flowering, the compost is allowed to dry out completely and the round tuber may be taken from the pot and cleaned off. Repot the following March using a peat-based compost and keep at 68°F (20°C) if possible. When growth commences, the temperature may be lowered to 60°F (15°C).

Seed sown in January or February at a temperature of 68°F (20°C) will produce plants to flower the following July. Healthy leaves cut into strips and inserted in peaty compost will root and grow new plants.

Hibiscus (Rose mallow; Marsh mallow) These very prolific plants from Africa and Asia produce magnificent flowers ranging from white through apricot, to pink and red. Some plants have single flowers and others double, but all are bright. *Hibiscus waimeae* has giant white flowers up to 6 inches (15 cm) across.

H. rosa-sinensis is the kind usually grown, and to keep its healthy dark green leaves the plant requires good light and a temperature above 50°F (10°C). Leaf fall is a sure sign that the plant is too cold. Sudden changes in growing conditions sometimes cause the flower buds to drop. The plant soon recovers however.

The pot compost should be moist from April to September and just moist for the other months. Continuous flowering takes a good deal of energy from the plant and a feed each week during active growth is beneficial.

Pruning in February by cutting the growths made last year back to three buds will keep the plant within bounds. New plants are easy to produce from cuttings.

Hippeastrum (Barbados lily) The South American plant is sometimes wrongly called Amaryllis. Spectacular trumpet-shaped flowers grow from the large potted bulb after Christmas and into the new year; the flower stalk tends

Left: Gloxinias produce bright flowers with a velvety texture.

Above: Prune the stems back to three buds in February and *Hibiscus* will produce a fine show of flowers.

to be very brittle so some care is needed when handling the plant.

Cool conditions with a minimum temperature of 50°F (10°C) will prolong flowering and the compost should be kept moist without being too wet. A feed each week when the plant is making active growth is a good investment because the plant may be grown from year to year.

Watering may be reduced during August, and when the leaves wither they are removed from the bulb. The bulb is given a good soak with clear water towards the end of October and if necessary put into a larger pot. There should be a 1-inch (25-mm) gap between the bulb and side of the pot with at least half of the bulb protruding from the compost.

37

Hoya (Wax flower; Porcelain flower; Honey plant) This climbing plant from India and Australia is best grown in a pot and trained on wire hoops. The waxy flowers look almost unreal and secrete tears of sugary nectar to attract insects. *Hoya bella* produces pinkish flowers with red or purple centres; *Hoya carnosa* is equally attractive with a mass of white flowers from May to November.

Good natural light shaded from strong sun is needed and the plant pot should be kept on the dry side from October to March.

New plants may be grown by cutting up the stem and inserting in peat-based compost. The plants are then grown on in a temperature of at least 50°F (10°C).

Hydrangea *H. macrophylla* is typically Japanese with its ball of papery bracts

The waxy *Hoya* flowers look almost unreal and secrete sugary nectar.

surrounding the minute flowers. It is very important to keep the pot compost moist when leaves are present, otherwise they will turn yellow and small flowers will result. After flowering, the pots are better stood outside or preferably the plant removed from the pot and planted in the garden.

Cuttings are taken in July or August from shoots which have no flower buds. An ideal cutting is approximately 3 inches (7·5 cm) long and cut across the stem below a leaf joint. The bottom pair of leaves are removed and it may be necessary to reduce the length of the next pair by cutting across the leaf. The base of the cutting should be dipped into rooting hormone powder to help promote root action.

Sulphate of alumina may be purchased from garden stores to add to the compost. This helps the plant to produce blue coloured bracts which are more attractive than those often produced naturally. Clean rain water is better than mains water because it is slightly acid and these are the conditions the plant requires for healthy growth.

Hydrangeas are better for keeping in cool conditions with good light, shaded from direct sun. The plant should be given a feed each week when in active growth. Flower heads look very attractive when they are cut and dried, then used for flower arrangements.

Jacobinia These plants grow to 5–6 ft (1·5–1·8 m) tall in their natural surroundings in Brazil but are likely to be much smaller in the home. *J. carnea* has a spike of pink flowers, whereas *J. coccinea* has scarlet red. The plants like to be in a light place with a minimum temperature of 55°F (13°C). Water the plant well from May to September and give it a feed of house plant food each week.

Pruning will help to keep the plant within bounds and is best done by cutting back the previous year's growth to 4 inches (10 cm) each March. When the resulting shoots grow, they may have the tips pinched out to promote branching and encourage more flowers.

Propagation is easy by taking cuttings in late May.

Kalanchoe (Star blossom; Flaming Katy) Star blossom is a very apt name given to this plant which grows naturally in South America, Africa and Asia. *K.*

blossfeldiana has small star-shaped flowers and thick, fleshy leaves.

Do not overwater the pot, especially during the cold dark months; the plant appreciates a feed every other week from May to September. Keep the plant in good natural light, otherwise the flowers tend to fade and the buds do not fully develop. Dead flowers should be removed to encourage further flowering. Nature has adapted the plant to cope with a dry atmosphere; it would be happy on a window sill above the radiator.

New plants can be raised from seed, although it is more usual to produce them by taking cuttings approximately 2 inches (5 cm) long. The plants are then grown on at 50°F (10°C) or above.

Pruning during March will keep *Jacobinia* within bounds.

39

Given a warm sunny position, Passion flowers may produce fruit as well.

Passiflora (Passion flower) The flowers produced by this climbing plant from Brazil look almost unreal. The plant is best provided with a wire hoop to cling to, or the pot may be placed in a basket with a large hoop handle.

Given a warm, sunny situation *P. caerulea* produces attractive flowers and fruits may develop too, although they are not very palatable. *P. edulis* is more likely to grow fruits worth eating.

Passiflora is not very fussy about temperature during the resting stage from November to March as long as it is free from frost.

Primula (Fairy primrose) *P. malacoides* is an easy grower and produces its bright flowers during the often dull months through October to March. Primulas like to be kept cool when they are growing and at 50°F (10°C) or just above when flowering. This Chinese plant revels in a moist atmosphere, which can be provided by standing the pot on a dish of moist pebbles.

Fairy primroses are usually raised from seed sown in June or July each year. Peat-based compost suits them well and it should be kept moist. When the pot is full of roots, house plant food will be required each week.

Saintpaulia (African violet) No wonder *S. ionantha* from Africa is the most popular flowering house plant. It is very attractive with a good colour range, will live for a number of years producing flowers for several months of the year and is easy to propagate. Remove a healthy leaf complete with stalk, then reduce the length of the stalk to ½ inch (12 mm) long and insert in a peat-based compost up to the bottom of the leaf. When small plants appear at the surface of the compost, they should be carefully removed and potted singly in 3-inch (7·5-cm) pots. Provided the temperature is never allowed to drop below 60°F (15°C), the new plants will flower in six months time. New plants may also be raised from seed sown on peat.

African violets should always be watered by immersing the pot in another container: should water touch the leaves they invariably mark with silvery white rings, often called ghost spots. The plants like humidity and a light place shaded from sunlight. Insufficient light is usually the reason for the lack of flowers, although temperatures below 60°F (15°C) can prevent flower buds from developing. The plants should be fed each week from April to September.

Spathiphyllum (White sails; Peace lily) An unusual and attractive plant from tropical America, the white sail-like flowers turn green after a while but they are still enchanting. *S. wallisii* is not usually more than 18 inches (46 cm) high and produces a profuse number of spathe-like flowers.

The plant likes to be kept in semi-shade, with humid conditions and moist roots. Move the plant on to a larger container in April or May. The plant may be divided up at the same time if new ones are required.

Streptocarpus (Cape primrose) *S. x hybridus* from South Africa has produced many fine varieties like the prolific blue flowered 'Constant Nymph', itself used to breed other interesting plants. Flowers appear from April through to November.

The plant appreciates shading from strong sun and the large leaves take up vast amounts of water during warm weather, so the compost should be kept on the moist side.

Seed may be sown to produce new plants, or a leaf can be cut into strips and inserted into compost. Small plants will form wherever veins have been severed: the young plants are then potted up singly and grown on in a temperature of 50°F (10°C) or more.

Below: African violets should be kept away from strong sun for best results.

Left: The thirsty Cape primrose flowers over a long period from April to November.

Section 2: Foliage House Plants

Adiantum (Maidenhair fern; Venus' hair fern) The leaves resemble thin scales of chocolate used to decorate trifles, except they are an attractive shade of green. The plant is everlasting and when older leaves eventually turn yellow they should be cut away. A humid atmosphere will prevent the leaves from shrivelling and although an occasional misting over with clear water is beneficial it is better to avoid spraying with an insecticide.

The plant thrives on clean rain water and the compost should be kept moist but not too wet. Feed the pot with house plant food every other week when growth is active from April to August. There are two things which cannot be endured: direct sunlight and draught. Shaded light without being too dark and snug warmth similar to its sub-tropical home are called for, although the plant is found growing wild in temperate areas too and will be happy provided the temperature does not fall below 55°F (12°C).

When more plants are needed, a good way to increase them is to carefully divide the root and pot up the pieces singly. May is a good time so that the divisions establish quickly.

Ananas (Pineapple) This is a splendid plant with its long strap-like leaves. The fruits of *Ananas comosus* are edible but it is unlikely that the pineapples will ripen properly in temperatures below 90°F (33°C). Even though this tropical American may not provide homegrown fruit, it is still well worth growing and likes to be no cooler than 60°F (15°C). There is also a variegated leaf form known as *Ananas comosus* 'Variegatus' with bright yellow stripes. Pineapple plants will eventually grow to 3 ft 3 in (1 m) tall and as wide; no doubt by then young suckers will have grown from the root area of the older plant. They may be carefully removed after taking the rootball from the pot to grow on separately.

Another way to propagate plants is to cut off the tuft of leaves together with a portion of the woody material from the top of a ripe fruit. With any luck, roots will eventually grow from the base, provided the section has been placed on a container of moist sand which should be kept warm.

Pineapple plants like a position where there is good natural light. This is especially important for the variegated kind, otherwise the coloured stripes turn dull.

Asparagus (Asparagus fern) Most plants communicate if only we take the trouble to try to understand them. The Asparagus fern is no exception: when the atmosphere is too dry, the fern goes brown; when the young shoots are yellow and do not turn green, the plant is too cold. This South African plant will tolerate temperatures as low as 45°F (7°C).

So elegant is the foliage of *Asparagus plumosus*, that it is often used for floral arrangements. Certainly it would adorn any light position shaded from strong sunlight. The plant likes plenty of water during the period of active growth from April to September, with the compost just moist during the months of October to March. House plant food given every other week in spring and summer will help to foster healthy growth.

New plants are raised from seed sown any time between March and May at a temperature of 68°F (20°C), or the roots of the plant may be knocked from the

A humid atmosphere will help to prevent the delicate leaves of Maidenhair fern from shrivelling.

The variegated Pineapple plant has bright strap-like leaves.

43

flower pot, divided and potted up using a peat-based or John Innes compost.

Aspidistra (Cast iron plant; Parlour palm) There can hardly be a less uncomplaining plant than the aptly named Cast iron plant. Tolerant of shade and temperatures down to 45°F (7°C), it prefers the airy conditions which were endured before the age of central heating to those now often found in the home.

The compost is best kept moist but not too wet, particularly from October to March, otherwise the leaves turn yellow and spotted. The wide strap-like leaves tend to attract dust and deserve to be wiped over from time to time with a damp cloth, or leaf shine products can be obtained from garden centres and stores to clean and put a sheen on the leaves.

Aspidistra elatior is a plant found in China; it has green leaves and there is also a variegated kind now available which is rapidly gaining favour.

When the plant gets too big for the container, it may be potted on to a larger size or divided up.

Begonia (Begonia rex) Insignificant flowers are more than compensated for by superbly marked leaves. In fact it is better to remove the flower buds as they appear so that the plant's energy is directed towards making more foliage.

These begonias originated in southeast Asia. They like to be kept warm with a temperature of at least 60°F (15°C), in a light position but shaded from strong sunlight. Peaty compost which is never allowed to dry out promotes good growth and a weekly feed during summer sustains the plant. An occasional spray over the leaves with clear water quickly freshens them up.

Well grown plants will be looking for a move into a larger pot each April or May time and there can be no doubt that a peaty compost suits them best of all.

New plants are produced by leaf sections and the best leaves to use are those that are almost fully grown and healthy. Remove the leaf from the plant complete with stalk; lay it flat on a clean surface and with a sharp knife cut into strips 1-inch (2·5-cm) wide. Then insert the strips edge first into peat-based compost so that $\frac{5}{8}$ inch (1·5 cm) is protruding above the level of the compost. The cuttings are then less likely to shrivel up than when they are simply placed flat on the surface.

The rooting container may be placed in a closed polythene bag or plant propagator. Provided a temperature of at least 60°F (15°C) is maintained, small roots will grow from the cut veins in the leaf, followed by shoots. When these are large enough to handle, they can be potted off singly in small pots, again using peat-based compost.

Chamaedorea elegans (Parlour palm) This small indoor palm from Mexico is also known as *Neanthe bella*. It is so elegant that it will fit in anywhere and will put up with draughts and poor light, although it will react strongly to direct sun.

Notice how the leaves brighten up when they are syringed over: the Parlour palm revels in humidity and it pays to stand the pot on a container filled with moist pebbles. Keep the water level below the surface of the pebbles, otherwise the water may find its way into the root zone of the plant.

Opposite page: The Cast iron plant is tolerant of a wide range of growing conditions.

Remove the flower buds of *Begonia rex* as they appear so that its energy will be directed into the leaves. The plant is easily grown from leaf cuttings.

Spider plants have attractive striped leaves and produce runners with young plants on the end.

Feed every week from May to August; the compost should be just moist all the year round. The plant is not too fussy about temperature; a minimum of 55°F (13°C) suits it well although it will not sulk below that from time to time.

Chlorophytum (Spider plant; St. Bernard's lily) A go-anywhere beginner's plant from South Africa. Known as *Chlorophytum elatum*, *C. comosum* or *C. capense*, it will be just as happy sitting on the edge of the bath as it will in the kitchen or elsewhere shaded from direct sunlight.

The thin strap-like leaves with their bright creamy white stripe are complemented by long stems terminating in small plants resembling spiders suspended by a silk thread. The daughter plants send out minute roots when the atmosphere is warm and humid; they may be pinched from the stem and potted up or left on the parent.

Feed every week during the months of April to August but avoid overwatering from September to April, otherwise brown marks will appear on the leaves. A minimum temperature of 45°F (7°C) is acceptable.

Cissus (Kangaroo vine) This plant from Australia grows in leaps and bounds. *Cissus antartica* is self supporting and provided with a frame would make a good screen plant given time; alternatively it can be used as a drooping plant.

46

The leaves tend to shrivel in a hot dry atmosphere: 50–60°F (10–15°C) with an occasional syringe over is ideal. The pot should be kept moist during April to September and only just moist from October to March, especially when the plant is in a cool place.

New Kangaroo vines are produced by nipping off the top 2 inches (5 cm) of the growing shoot, or cut through the portion of stem between each leaf so that each cutting has part of the stem, a leaf and a bud between the leaf stalk and stem. Roots grow faster when the base of the cutting is dipped into rooting hormone powder before inserting in a peat-based compost.

Codiaeum (Croton; Joseph's coat; South sea laurel) Not the easiest of plants to grow where cold and draughts are concerned because the leaves tend to drop off under those conditions. Where a temperature of at least 60°F (15°C) can be maintained the plant will grow to 2 ft 6 inches (60 cm) bearing bright splashes of many coloured leaves. The leaf colour tends to be brighter when the plant is placed in good light and shaded from strong sun.

This plant from south-east Asia prefers moist compost with a feed of house plant food every week from March to September. Regular misting over with clear water will freshen the leaves.

Coleus (Flame nettle) Yet another first rate plant originating in south-east Asia, *Coleus blumei* belongs to the nettle family, but it certainly does not sting. A single packet of seed will produce a selection of plants with a very wide assortment of leaf colour and shape. The choicest may then be used to propagate new plants and each one will produce the same type as its parent. Cuttings are very easy to root.

Alternatively a plant can be obtained from the garden centre or florist, but either way flower buds should be pinched out before they have a chance to develop, otherwise woody growth will follow and there is less chance of further shoot development. The flowers are rather insignificant and of little decorative value.

Side shoots are encouraged to grow and make a bushy shape by removing the growing tip when the plant is 6 inches (15 cm) tall; given the same treatment when the resulting growth is 6 inches long, the plant will be a magnificent show in a short space of time.

Loam-based compost often gives the best results with this particular plant: the leaves tend to be a more intense colour and the plant has a more compact habit. However, where peat compost is used a high potash tomato feed is better than house plant food to compensate for the lush growth peat often produces in

Bushy growth is encouraged by pinching out the stem tip. Few plant families offer such a wide variety of leaf colours as Flame nettles.

Earth star is a very apt name for a plant with such squat striped leaves.

the Flame nettle. A position in good light also enhances the leaf colour.

Cordyline (Club palm) Despite the fact that *Cordyline indivisia* originally came from Africa, it appreciates being shaded from strong sun: the long green leaves with their yellow or red markings will be all the better for it. The plant does like plenty of light during short days and it is important not to overwater then. Nevertheless, a moist compost is beneficial from May to September together with a feed every other week. The minimum temperature to aim for is 50°F (10°C).

New plants are raised from cuttings taken from the root in April or May, or by cutting up the stem into 1-inch (2·5-cm) lengths.

Cryptanthus (Earth star; Terrestrial star; Starfish bromeliad) The striped leaves really come into their own when the plant is placed in a light position; it likes to be shaded from strong sun and prefers to be kept warm around 60°F (15°C).

Cryptanthus bivittatus minor is a low growing plant and well suited to a bottle garden. Overwatering should be avoided at all times.

Cyperus (Umbrella plant) A very elegant plant from Africa, it will withstand temperatures down to 55°F (13°C) without coming to harm. *Cyperus alternifolius* is the choice when a tall plant is required because it grows to approximately 6 ft 6 inches (2 m) tall; *C. diffusus* is much shorter when fully grown at 2 ft (60 cm).

This marsh plant likes to have its roots moist at all times and so it is not a bad idea to place the flower pot in another container with water covering the bottom.

Umbrella plants are easy to germinate from seed, or cuttings may be taken by removing the 'umbrella' with 2 inches (5 cm) of stalk and inserting in moist peat up to the leaves.

Dieffenbachia (Dumb cane; Leopard lily) *D. picta* is a winner with its bright variegated leaves and the colour is better for keeping the plant in good light but shaded from strong sun. Originating in South America, the Dumb cane likes to be kept warm with a minimum temperature of 60°F (15°C); draughts should be avoided to prevent the leaves turning yellow.

A humid atmosphere is ideal and the compost should be moist, with a feed of house plant food every week during the period April to September. The plant looks forward to a rest from October to March when the pot compost is better on the dry side.

The flowers are rather insignificant and may be removed so that the energy will be used to produce more leaves. New plants grow up from the base of the parent and these 'toes' can be removed after carefully taking the original plant from its pot. Alternatively the parent plant stem may be cut up into small portions each with a leaf scar and bud. The stem cuttings are then inserted in John Innes Seed Compost or a mixture of peat and sand.

Care should be taken to wash the hands after touching the plant; the sap can have nasty consequences causing numbness of the tongue. That is why the plant was given the name Dumb cane.

Dracaena (Dragon tree) *D. deremensis* is one of the nicest Dragon trees with its dashing striped leaves, and in Africa and Asia will grow to 8 ft (2·5 m). Many years will pass before the plant outgrows its welcome indoors though. Even then the stem may be cut up into small sections to root for new plants.

A minimum temperature of 60°F (15°C) is required with a humid atmosphere during the warm, dry months, otherwise the leaf tips turn brown when the air is too dry. This problem may also be caused by using tap water with more than enough flourine.

The Dumb cane likes to be kept moist during warm weather, in a light place shaded from strong sun.

Right: Fat-headed Lizzie is a good plant to grow in poor light.

Below: Rubber plants are often more attractive when the main stem tip is removed to promote branching.

Dragon trees are hungry plants and look for a feed of house plant food every week from April to September. Watering and syringing leaves should be reduced in October until the following March.

Fatshedera (Fat-headed Lizzie) *x F. lizei* is a plant bred by crossing *Fatsia japonica* and the Irish ivy. Both parents are hardy outdoor plants although Fatshedera is better for being kept at around 45°F (7°C) or above. An easy plant to place because it will tolerate poor light.

New plants are produced by taking cuttings from the end of shoots, or the stem may be cut up so that each portion has a leaf and bud.

Ficus (Rubber plant) Another group of tolerant plants which are easy to grow. Poor light is not too much of a hindrance, although they prefer good light shaded from strong sun. Overwatering should be avoided, especially during the winter, and it is better to let the compost dry out slightly between applications.

Ficus elastica 'Decora' and 'Robusta' are inclined to grow tall quickly unless the top is snapped off. This causes the plant to grow side shoots. 'Black Prince' is a very attractive plant with dark bottle green leaves.

Ficus benjamina is a graceful weeping fig which will eventually grow to the ceiling. It appreciates a mist over with clear water from time to time. Dry compost should be avoided, otherwise the leaves tend to drop.

Ficus radicans 'Variegata' has small leaves and is rather unusual in that it has a creeping habit.

Ficus can be grown from seed although the seed must have light and a temperature of 80°F (25°C) to germinate. *F. elastica* can be propagated by air layering or by cutting the stem into portions, each with a leaf and bud. *F. benjamina* and *radicans* may be grown from cuttings.

Fittonia (Snake skin plant) *F. verschaffeltii* is rather more exacting in its requirements than the ivory-veined leaved form *F. argyroneura*. This interesting plant from Peru needs a temperature of at least 60°F (15°C), shade and humidity. It is an ideal plant for the bottle garden or terrarium.

The prostrate stems root themselves so propagation is simply a case of carefully cutting off the rooted portions.

Grevillea (Silk oak) This is another plant from Australasia which grows in leaps and bounds. Sow some Silk oak seeds today and within a year the elegant pot trees will be 4 ft 6 inches (1·5 m) tall. Grevilleas are particularly good in groups of plants, their deeply cut leaves filtering light through to those below. They are very easy plants to grow, given a light, cool and draught-free position.

Hedera (Ivy) The Ivy family consists of an extraordinary number of plants with fascinating leaves: some have tiny arrow-head shapes, others like *Hedera helix* 'Cristata' are crinkled. The very large, shiny leaved *H. helix* 'Canariensis' has a yellow flash.

These plants from Europe and the Canary Islands are very tolerant of poor growing conditions, although the variegated leaved kinds do better in good light. They like low temperatures, tolerating almost freezing conditions.

The pot compost should be kept moist for the months of April to September and on the dry side for the remainder of the year. House plant food given each week from May to September will help the plant to grow well, and an occasional mist over the leaves is appreciated.

Propagation is simply a case of cutting the stems up with a pair of scissors and inserting each piece, complete with leaf and bud into a pot of compost.

House plant food given each week from May to September will help to keep Ivy growing well. The variegated kinds like good light.

Kentia (Howea; Paradise palm) Very elegant palm reminiscent of shimmering paradise islands. In fact they are extremely easy to grow and will come to no harm in a temperature as low as 50°F (10°C). The plants tolerate shade and are slow growing. Moist compost with a feed each week from May to September is beneficial; the compost should be just moist for the remainder of the year.

Kentia belmoreana tends to be more relaxed in growth than *K. fosteriana*, otherwise they are very similar. The plants can be raised from seed.

Maranta (Prayer plant) Another interesting plant from tropical America, the maranta is called Prayer plant

Provided the Cheese plant is kept away from draughts, it will be happy in most positions in the home.

because the leaves fold together towards the end of the day.

M. leuconeura 'Erythrophylla' is a vigorous low growing plant; when its prostrate stems stray too far they may be used as cuttings.

The plant likes shade and is well suited to growing in a terrarium at a temperature around 60°F (15°C).

Monstera (Swiss cheese plant; Bread plant) A favourite in many homes because it tolerates a wide range of growing conditions, although the Cheese plant dislikes draughts which cause the leaves to develop brown spots. Good light shaded from strong sun is desired, otherwise the leaf stalks become ungainly through reaching out for light.

Low temperatures around 50°F (10°C) often produce lanky plants with spindly stems, small leaves with few holes and slits. Higher temperatures near 70°F (20°C) encourage a bushy habit and larger leaves with slits and holes.

Aerial roots grow from the leaf joints and they should be tucked into the pot rather than being cut off, when they usually only grow again. The plant pot should be given house plant food every ten days during the growing period from April to September.

New plants can be raised from seed or by cuttings.

Peperomia (Peper elder) Tropical America gave us this plant with a most unusual flower which is colourless. Clustered together on their stalk they resemble a rat's tail. The beauty of the plant is in its bun shape and with *P. caperata*, the crinkled leaves; there is also a variegated form of *P. caperata*.

These plants have very closely packed crowns in the pot and so are better watered from below. A temperature of 55°F (13°C) is satisfactory.

New plants may be raised in a rather novel way by snapping off a leaf with its stalk. The stalk is reduced so that $\frac{1}{2}$ inch (12 mm) remains with the leaf; the leaf stalk is then inserted into a peat-based compost and roots will grow from the base. Small plants will eventually push up through the compost to grow on. The same method can be used with *P. caperata* 'Variegata' although the young plants will be green. The only way to retain the variegation with that plant is to divide the parent.

Philodendron (Sweetheart plant) *P. scandens* from tropical America gets its common name from the heart-shaped leaves. The long stems are often trained up a frame, or they may hang over the edge of the flower pot. Humidity is appreciated so the leaves should be damped over in dry spells. Sudden changes in temperature should be avoided, as should strong sunlight.

Sweetheart plants are at their best in a warm place around 55°F (13°C) and shaded from strong sun. Whilst the compost needs to be kept moist from April to September, less water will be required from October to March.

Propagation is by cuttings taken from the end of the shoot, or by sections of stem with a leaf and bud.

Phoenix (Palm) *P. robelenii* usually produces a more attractive plant than *P. canariensis* although they both make splendid pot plants. They are similar to the commercial date palms, although they are unlikely to produce miniature date fruits in the home, as they do in their native Asia and in the Canary Islands.

The palms are easy to grow from seed, and when they germinate the plants may be grown on in a minimum temperature of 50°F (10°C).

Pilea (Aluminium plant) A good beginners plant because it is tolerant of a wide range of growing conditions. Ideally, it should be kept above 50°F (10°C) in good light but shaded from strong sun. *P. cadierei* tends to grow rather straggly unless the growths are pinched from time to time to induce side branching and a bushy habit.

The Aluminium plant from tropical America derives its common name from the silvery specks in the leaf. Cuttings root readily and are snapped 2 inches (5 cm) long from the plant. They are then inserted into peat-based compost, four cuttings to each 3-inch (7·5-cm) pot.

Platycerium (Stag's horn fern; Elk's horn fern) *P. bifurcatum* produces two types of frond: one clings to the support and resembles flat plates, the other looks like a stag's antler. These plants from Africa and Australia are fascinating because they do not have roots that grow in soil; the plants attach themselves to a tree instead, although they are not parasites. Moisture and debris is collected in the fronds to nourish the plant.

Stag's horn ferns are patient plants and are happy with a temperature of 50°F (10°C) with an occasional spray over with tepid water.

Polypodium (Hare's foot fern) *P. aureum* produces prostrate stems not unlike hare's feet. These unusual furry growths cover the surface of the container with time and although unusual and decorative, the pot is then best watered by immersing in another container.

Despite the fact that the plant originated in the West Indies, it will tolerate a temperature as low as 45°F (7°C).

Rhoicissus (Grape ivy) The growth habit of this South African provides the opportunity to use it as a room divider. *R. rhomboidea*, also known as *Cissus rhombifolia*, grows tendrils so that it is able to cling to a support. It will grow to 9 ft 9 inches (3 m) if allowed to have its own way, although the plant can be kept smaller by pinching out the leading growths or by training on a smaller support.

Grape ivy leaves are an attractive shape and glossy. They appreciate a damp over from time to time and protection from strong sun. Moist compost is beneficial, although overwatering should be avoided, especially during the months of October to March. April to September is the time of active growth, when house plant food is needed each week.

Cuttings are easy to root and the plants benefit from being given a home in good natural light with a minimum temperature of 45°F (7°C).

Sanservieria (Mother-in-law's tongue)

S. trifasciata is the sharp one from West Africa; the leaves are strap-like and pointed too. *S.t.* 'Laurentii' has a yellow stripe along the margin each side of the leaf. A very popular plant and useful for those people who forget to water their plants because it is suitable for hot, dry centrally heated rooms. The pot is better kept dry from September to March to avoid rotting at the stem base; then as the longer days approach moist warm conditions will encourage flowering. Let the compost dry out before watering again. A feed each week from May to September will help to keep the plant growing well and a minimum temperature of 50°F (10°C) is all that is required.

Propagate new plants by removing a leaf and then cutting across to make several strips 2 inches (5 cm) long. The leaf portions are stuck vertically into compost and will root, new plants growing from the base. Although 'Laurentii' will root and produce new plants they will be without the yellow margins. The best way to propagate 'Laurentii' to keep its stripes is to knock the rootball from its pot and cut off a sucker or 'toe', that is a small plant growing from the parent root.

Saxifraga (Mother of Thousands)

Here is an interesting little plant from China: *S. stolonifera* was given its name

because it is forever producing daughter plants on the end of runner stems. The leaves are round and green, although the very decorative 'Tricolour' has red and white in the leaf too.

An ideal plant for suspended pots, it is happy in cool temperatures down to 45°F (7°C) provided the compost is not wet. New plants are easily grown by pinching off the young ones from the end of the stolons.

Schefflera (Umbrella plant)

S. actinophylla from Australia is an elegant plant with leaves like open palms on the end of long stalks. *S. arboricula* is more dwarf and the glossy dark green leaves are very attractive.

Draughts or temperature below 50°F (10°C) will cause brown patches to appear on the leaves; otherwise it is an

The strap-like leaves of Mother-in-law's tongue are happy in the dry atmosphere of a centrally heated room.

Wandering Jew is a very good plant for hanging pots.

easy enough plant to grow, provided the compost is kept moist and the pot is given a feed each week from April to September.

Seed sown in spring will germinate to make fine plants within six months.

Scindapsus (Devil's ivy) The heart-shaped leaves can be mistaken for those of *Philodendron* and although similar in many ways, Devil's ivy originated in Asia. *S. aureus* 'Golden Queen' usually has a good deal of yellow in the leaf, whereas 'Marble Queen' has white instead.

Dry air causes the leaves to curl up and turn yellow – a mist over with water from time to time is appreciated. Keep the plant shaded from strong sun and avoid overwatering. The trailing stems look very attractive when they are tied to a stick pushed into the pot and covered with moss.

New plants can be made by cutting the stem into portions, each with a bud and leaf.

Tradescantia and Zebrina (Wandering Jew) These trailing plants from tropical America are so easy to grow that they are often underrated. Yet they are useful in so many ways: trailing over the side of a room divider or shelf, or perhaps suspended from a container.

Light shade is preferable as the leaves tend to scorch when they are subjected to very strong sunlight. After a while the stems may become lanky and devoid of leaves; before that happens it would be as well to pinch off the end 2 inches (5 cm) of the shoots and insert them in a glass of water to root. Alternatively cuttings may be inserted directly into the flower pot because rooting is easy and quick.

Grow the plants on in a temperature of at least 50°F (10°C) with plenty of water during active growth. A feed each week from April to September will help to keep the growth healthy. Pinching out the shoot tip from time to time will stimulate bushy growth.

Section 3: Flowering or Foliage House Plants

Abutilon (Flowering maple; Indian maple; Chinese bellflower) This is a delightful plant producing a mass of bellshaped flowers from March to October. Allow plenty of room because it can grow 6–7 ft (2m) tall. There is also the kind with yellow flecks in the leaves known as *Abutilon striatum* 'Thompsonii'. Both can tolerate temperatures down to 40°F (5°C) and prefer to be kept cool,

Flowering maple is a delightful plant producing a mass of bellshaped flowers.

otherwise they become thin and straggly. These plants revel in outdoor conditions during the warmer months of June to August.

Keep the roots moist by regular watering when flower buds appear and a feed with house plant food once every two weeks will be appreciated during the flowering period. Reduce watering in October until the following April so that the compost is only just moist; liquid feed may be given once a month from October to March.

New plants can be raised from seed, or soft shoots taken from the existing plant will produce roots when they are inserted in a flower pot filled with a peat-based compost. April or May is the best time to take cuttings and they should be approximately 3 inches (7·5 cm) long.

Aechmea (Urn plant) This fascinating plant lives as an epiphyte attached to the side of a tree in its natural surroundings in the southern half of America. The centre of the plant has been shaped like a funnel or urn, so that when rain falls, it is trapped and made use of by the plant. Leaves and insects are also caught from time to time and eventually dissolve to provide nourishment. Urn plants in the house are usually grown in a flower pot. They still like to be watered by keeping the urn topped up and a monthly feed of house plant food helps to keep the plant happy.

Flower heads last for several months and when the last of the actual mauve-coloured flowers has faded, it is best to cut away the flower stem and coloured leaf-like bracts of the head.

Aechmeas are inclined to rot off at the base of the stem when the pot compost is kept moist or if the temperature drops

Left: Urn plants should be watered in the funnel otherwise the stem base is inclined to rot when the pot compost is too wet.

Below: Frequent watering is necessary to keep the Zebra plant happy and the flower stems should be cut back when the flowers fade.

below 56°F (13°C) for any length of time. Otherwise it is easy to grow and a long-lived member of the family, growing to around 2 ft (60 cm) tall.

Young plants will grow from the base of the parent and when they are 6 inches (15 cm) high, they may be carefully removed from the main root.

Aphelandra (Zebra plant) Chinese architects could have taken the flowering head of aphelandra for inspiration when designing the first pagoda; the yellow spike remains after the true tubular flowers have fallen. When the actual flowers have finished, the stems may be cut back to leave two pairs of good leaves on each branch. This will encourage the plant to produce new growth which will eventually flower. The stems that have been cut off can be made into leaf bud cuttings, each portion of stem with its own leaf and bud. Since the leaves are opposite, the cutting is cut down the middle to make two.

Despite first being found in tropical America, the Zebra plant is happy provided it is in a temperature of 50°F (10°C); in fact if too hot the leaves become distorted and so it is better to keep below 70°F (20°C). The Zebra plant loves a moist root run so the compost should be watered freely. Humidity is important to avoid brown spots appearing on the leaves and shading from bright sun is beneficial too.

59

Aphelandra squarrosa 'Louisae' is a well-known variety growing to 2 ft (60 cm) tall, and has attractive markings on the leaves. *A.s.* 'Dania' is similar although more compact.

Billbergia (Queen's tears) Many plants are named after people and this one is no exception. Found in South America, billbergia derives its name from Gustaf Johannes Billberg, a Swedish botanist. The leaves look similar to those of the Pineapple plant, although smaller. This plant grows no more than approximately 1 ft (30 cm) tall and as wide.

Billbergia nutans is very easy to grow, tolerates a dry atmosphere and likes to be placed in good light. Provided it is fed every other week when flower buds appear in April or May and the compost kept moist until September, each year brings forth the weeping flower stems with the bright pink bracts.

Billbergia can withstand the cold months as long as the compost is on the dry side; no harm will be done when the temperature falls a degree or so below 50°F (10°C).

Citrus (Calamondin orange) *Citrus mitis* from the Philippines makes a delightful miniature tree. It produces edible although rather bitter fruits and there is just something about flavouring a drink with an orange slice from your own tree; homemade marmalade is good too. The flowers are very fragrant and they alone justify growing the plant, although fruits often set after the flowers have been lightly dusted over with a soft paint brush or piece of cotton wool.

Seed will germinate at 60°F (15°C) and the plant likes to be grown on in much the same temperature. Plants will also grow from cuttings taken in June or July and they root better when a small heel of harder stem remains on the base of the cutting. Orange plants like plenty of light; a bright window or sun room is ideal. Overwatering causes the leaves to go yellow so just sufficient is required to stop the pot compost from drying out. Watering every three days from June to August, with a feed every other week should be just right.

Columnea *Columnea x banksii* is a trailing plant from Central America and the mass of bright red flowers give warmth to cold days. In fact the flowering period extends from November through to the following April.

This plant is at home in a temperature of 55°F (13°C) and above and looks very attractive in a suspended pot or hanging basket. It is an easy grower and cuttings taken in May or June are eager to root.

Billbergia looks like a miniature pineapple plant and it is very easy to grow.

The bright red flowers of
Columnea give warmth to cold
winter days.

Cyclamen *Cyclamen persicum* from Syria gets more popular every year, and rightly so, because it is one of the best flowering house plants available, with a range of flower colours and patterned leaves.

A temperature of around 50–60°F (10–15°C) is ideal; anything much above will cause the flower stems and leaves to go soft and floppy and the plant to take on an altogether unhealthy appearance. The plant likes a light position otherwise the leaves turn yellow.

Stand the pot in a container of water when the pot compost feels dry to the touch. This avoids water collecting around the leaf and flower stalks which may cause rotting. A feed each week will be appreciated while the plant is making active growth.

New plants may be raised each year from seed and the traditional time to sow is in August or January. There is no reason why seed should not be sown at any time except that the plants usually start to flower in September, and the seed sown from February to July will not really have a chance to grow into very large plants by the time they flower.

Dry Cyclamen off after flowering to give them a rest and they will grow and flower again the following year. The corms will last for many years given good treatment.

The plant grows best in peat-based compost at a temperature of 55°F (13°C) or above. Three cuttings to a 3-inch (7·5-cm) pot will soon root and make a fine display in warm conditions.

Impatiens (Busy Lizzie) Although the plant is happy in a temperature of 45°F (7°C), gentle heat will provide suitable conditions for the plant to produce flowers all the year round.

This African plant likes moist roots with a feed every ten days. Good light shaded from strong sun is ideal.

Cuttings snapped from the plant and inserted in peat-based compost or water root easily, or seed may be sown to raise new plants.

Nerium (Oleander) A nicely shaped plant with small strap-like leaves and pinkish flowers, the nerium will eventually make a small bushy tree up to 9 ft (2·7 m) high in its native Mediterranean region. The plant likes good natural light, moist compost and a minimum temperature of 50°F (10°C).

Cuttings will root provided they have been taken with a small sliver or heel of mature stem in June or July. Plants may also be raised from seed sown from March to May.

Rhipsalidopsis (Easter cactus) Often known as *Zygocactus*, the Easter cactus is ideal for hanging baskets and produces its flowers during April to June. The flowers are purple red in colour and rather smaller than the Christmas cactus. The flat stems are easily propagated by snapping from the plant and inserting in sandy compost.

The Easter cactus from Central and South America should be allowed to go dry during October and November so that flower buds are initiated. Start watering when buds begin to emerge and the plant may then be given a feed of house plant food every other week.

Ricinus (Castor oil plant) An African plant, *Ricinus communis* produces large leaves and attractive prickly seed pods. The plants are best grown afresh each year by sowing the bean-like patterned seed in March or April.

The plants grow really fast and require plenty of water and plant food. Pot on into a larger pot when the present one is full of roots. Castor oil plants tolerate cool conditions, down to a minimum of 45°F (7°C).

The same plant can be grown for several years: dry the plant off after flowering by withholding water. When the leaves die down they should be removed complete with stalk. Restart growth in July by watering the compost and when leaves appear the plant should be moved on into a slightly larger size pot. When potting cyclamen keep most of the round corm above the level of the compost: the plant will flower sooner and growth will be faster.

Hypocyrta (Clog plant) *H. radicans* from tropical America has small glossy green leaves and numerous bright orange clog-shaped flowers. It is ideal for hanging pots and baskets.

Left: Busy Lizzie likes moisture at the roots and will flower all year round.

Left: Busy Lizzie likes moisture at the roots and will flower all year round.

Below: Provided the roots are kept on the dry side from October for a month, the Easter cactus will flower during April to June.

Schlumbergera (Christmas cactus)

S. x buckleyi is also known as *Zygocactus truncatus*; it is often confused with the Easter cactus by nature of its late flowering in some years. Christmas cactus requires more hours of darkness than light in each 24-hour period from the beginning of September to ensure flowers for Christmas. Warmth is important too and a temperature of at least 65°F (18°C) is required to produce flowers at that time, otherwise the plant is happy enough with 60°F (15°C).

Avoid very dry conditions during flowering otherwise the buds will drop. After flowering, reduce watering so that the plant goes nearly dry and rest it until May. Regular watering can begin again with a feed each week. A dry period through July and August would help to start flower bud production.